RETURN TO THE FORBIDDEN PLANET

by Bob Carlton

A SAMUEL FRENCH ACTING EDITION

SAMUEL FRENCH

FOUNDED 1830

New York Hollywood London Toronto

SAMUELFRENCH.COM

RETURN TO THE FORBIDDEN PLANET MUSICAL NUMBERS

WIPEOUT by Patrick Connolly, Robert Berryhill, James Fuller, Ronald Wilson © 1963 (Miraleste Music & Robin Hood Music Co.)

IT'S A MAN'S WORLD by James Brown, Betty Newsome © 1966 (Unichappel Music, Inc.)

GREAT BALLS OF FIRE by Otis Blackwell, Jack Hammer © 1957 (Chappell & Co. and Unichappel Music, Inc.)

DON'T LET ME BE MISUNDERSTOOD by Gloria Caldwell, Sol Marchus, Bennie Benjamin © 1964 & 1965 (Bennie Benjamin Music, Inc., admin. by Chappell & Co.)

GOOD VIBRATIONS by Brian Wilson, Mike Love © 1966 (Irving Music, Inc.)

THE SHOOP SHOOP SONG by Rudy Clark © 1963 & 1964 (Alley Music Corporation and Trio Music, Inc.)

I'M GONNA CHANGE THE WORLD by Eric Burdon © (Rightsong Music, Inc.)

A TEENAGER IN LOVE? by Doc Pomus, Mort Shuman © 1959 (Unichappel Music, Inc.)

YOUNG GIRL by Jerry Fuller © 1968 (Warner-Tamerlane Publishing Corp.)

SHE'S NOT THERE by Rod Argent © 1964 (Marquis Music Co., Ltd./Al Gallico Music Corp.)

SHAKIN' ALL OVER by Johnny Kidd © 1960 (Mills Music, Inc.)

GLORIA by Van Morrison © 1965 (Unichappel Music, Inc.)

WHO'S SORRY NOW? by Bert Kalmar, Harry Ruby, Ted Snyder © 1923 (Mills Music, Inc.)

TELL HER by Bert Russell © 1953 (Screen Gems-EMI Music Inc.)

OH, PRETTY WOMAN by Roy Orbison, Bill Dees © 1964 (Acuff-Rose Publications, Inc.)

ROBOT MAN by Sylvia Dee, George Goehring © 1960 (Chappell & Co.)

SHAKE, RATTLE AND ROLL by Charles Calhoun © 1954 (Unichappel Music, Inc.)

GO NOW by Larry Banks, Milton Bennett © 1963 (Trio Music Co., Inc. admin. by Unichappell Music)

ONLY THE LONELY by Roy Orbison, Joe Melson © 1960 (Acuff-Rose Publications, Inc.)

BORN TO BE WILD Mars Bonfire © 1968 (Music Corp. of America)

MISTER SPACEMAN Roger McGuinn © 1966 (Tickson Music)

MONSTER MASH by Bobby Pickett, Leonard Capizzi © 1962, 1973 (Acoustic Music, Inc.)

IMPORTANT BILLING AND CREDIT REQUIREMENTS

All producers of RETURN TO THE FORBIDDEN PLANET *must* give credit to the Author and Composer of the Play in all programs distributed in connection with performances of the Play and in all instances in which the title of the Play appears for purposed of advertising, publicizing or otherwise exploiting the Play and/or a production. The names of the Author *must* also appear on a separate line, on which no other name appears, immediately following the title, and must appear in a size of type not less than fifty percent of size of the title type. Billing must be substantially as follows:

(NAME OF PRODUCER)

PRESENTS

RETURN TO THE FORBIDDEN PLANET
by
BOB CARLTON

Further, all programs distributed in connection with performances of the Play are required to give credit as follows:

"Produced in 1991 at Variety Arts Theatre,
New York City"

Andre Ptaszynski and Don Taffner
present
RETURN TO THE FORBIDDEN PLANET
Written and Directed by
BOB CARLTON
with

Gabriel Barre	Allison Briner	Julee Cruise
Mary Ehlinger	Erin Hill	David LaDuca
Robert McCormick	Michael Rotondi	Steve Steiner
Chuck Tempo	Louis Tucci	James H. Wiggins, Jr.

RETURN TO THE FORBIDDEN PLANET
by
Bob Carlton

First London West End production opened at the
Cambridge Theatre,
September 11, 1989

Off-Broadway production opened at the
Variety Arts Theatre,
October 10, 1991.
N.Y. production produced by
Donald L. Taffner and Andre Ptanszynski

MUSICAL NUMBERS

ACT I

Wipeout
It's a Man's World
Great Balls of Fire
Don't Let Me Be Misunderstood
Good Vibrations
The Shoop Shoop Song
I'm Gonna Change the World
A Teenager in Love?
Young Girl
She's Not There
Shakin' All Over
Gloria

ACT II

Gloria (reprise)
Don't Let Me Be Misunderstood (reprise)
Who's Sorry Now?
Tell Her
She's Not There (underscore)
It's a Man's World (underscore and reprise)
Oh, Pretty Woman
It's a Man's World (underscore)
Robot Man
Shake, Rattle and Roll
Gloria (underscore)
Go Now
Don't Let Me Be Misunderstood (underscore)
Only the Lonely
Born to Be Wild
Mister Spaceman

Epilogue
The Monster Mash
Great Balls of Fire (reprise)

PRESHOW

(Fifteen minutes before the show starts members of the cast mingle with the audience. They welcome them aboard "Scientific Survey Flight Nine". A few minutes before the scheduled start to the show the crew take the audience through the regulation safety procedures. They point out the emergency exits, inform them that in the event of cabin depressurization oxygen masks will come down from overhead compartments etc. All the dialogue is improvised in character as 1950's "B" movie stereotypes. Finally the crew teach the audience the "Polarity Reversal Procedure".)

CREW. Finally, the polarity reversal drill. Polarity reversal is a very dangerous procedure. However, in the unlikely event of us entering a polarity reversal situation, we ask you to follow this simple drill. Please watch me closely.
Step one—put your hands in the air.

(They raise their hands in the air and encourage the audience to do likewise.)

Step two—place your hands on your cranium.

(They put their hands on their heads and encourage the audience to do likewise.)

Step three—exert pressure in a downwards motion.

(They press down on their heads and encourage the audience to do likewise.)

Step four—on the command "polarity reversed" equalize your external equilibrium by exhaling thus:

(They raise their hands in the air and exhale.)

(They take the audience through this one more time or until they have learned the drill.)

Thank you for your attention. Enjoy your flight.

(When F.O.H. clearance is given the COMPANY assemble on stage. CAPTAIN TEMPEST enters.)

BOSUN. Captain on the bridge!

(The CREW salute.)

TEMPEST. Carry on.

(THE VOYAGE BEGINS.)

ACT I

BOSUN. Friends, crewmen, passengers, lend me your ears.
Captain Tempest welcomes you aboard
This routine scientific survey flight.
TEMPEST. We hope you have a very pleasant trip.
But any questions that should come to mind,
Just ask our new Science Officer.
SCIENCE OFFICER.   That's me.
BOSUN. If there be truth in sight, she is a woman.
SCIENCE OFFICER. Think you I am no stronger than my sex?
Bosun, commence the pre-flight checks.

(Synthesizer effect.)

BOSUN.   Yes ma'am.
Check matrix.

(Synthesizer effect.)

BOSUN. Check.
SCIENCE OFFICER. Check all the photon shields.

(Synthesizer effect.)

BOSUN. Check.
SCIENCE OFFICER. Check the Dilithian Crystal rods.

(Synthesizer effect.)

BOSUN. Check.
SCIENCE OFFICER. The gravitational resistors.

9

(Synthesizer effect.)

BOSUN. Check.
SCIENCE OFFICER. And now check all the audio-visual screens.

(Blackout. The on-stage video screen comes on to reveal the newscaster. In the original production this part was played by the television astronomer Patrick Moore.)

NEWSCASTER. *(On video.)*
Two parents, both alike in dignity.
In outer space, where we our play locate,
From ancient grudge break to new mutiny,
And on Forbidden Planet meet their fate.
From forth the fatal loins of these two foes
A lovely star-borne daughter takes her life
Whose teenage crush and adolescent woes
Do drive her father mad and end his life.
The fearful passage of his death-marked love
And the continuance of her mother's rage,
Which but a monstrous end, naught could remove
Is now the two hours' traffic of our stage,
The which, if you with patient ears attend,
What here shall miss, our toil shall strive to mend.

(The video screen goes off.)

BOSUN. We have completed all the pre-flight checks.
TEMPEST. Commence countdown
NAVIGATIONAL OFFICER. 10, 9, 8, 7, 6, 5, 4, 3, 2, 1.
Ignition.
We have lift off.

(The CREW plays "Wipeout". The lights comes up, and the effect is of a space ship in action. On the video screen we see the ship lift off from the Earth and then it's flight through the galaxy. When "Wipeout" has established itself the following dialogue is spoken.)

BOSUN. All hail and welcome each and everyone.
Thank you for traveling with us today
On Interplanetary Space Flight Nine.
We're cruising now out into hyperspace,
And, as the Captain has switched off the sign
You may, of course, unclasp your safety belts.
Thank you.

("Wipeout" ends.)

TEMPEST. Ensign!
Make haste and take the bridge.
Cookie, go below.
Fetch us all the food and be quick.
Thou wert best to answer other business.
BOSUN. Shrug'st thou, malice?
If thou neglect'st or dost unwillingly
What I command, I'll put you in the brig.
SCIENCE OFFICER.*(To COOKIE.)* They want their porridge
and their fat full beaves
Either they must be dieted like mules
Or piteous they will look like drowned mice.

(COOKIE exits.)

TEMPEST. *(To BOSUN.)*
Yond' woman has a mean and hungry look,
She thinks too much: Women are dangerous.
BOSUN. Fear her not, Captain. She's not dangerous.
She is a noble doctor, and well given.
TEMPEST. Would she were flatter! But I fear her not.
Yet if my name were liable to fear
I do not know the woman I'd avoid
So soon as that Science Officer.
She reads much. She is a great observer,
And she looks quite through the deeds of men.
Women you see are never at hearts ease
Whilst they behold a greater than themselves
And therefore are they very dangerous.

(The intro of "It's a Man's World" underscores the following.)

SCIENCE OFFICER. I grant I am a woman, but withal
A woman well respected. It's on file.
TEMPEST. Fie fie! Unknit that threatening and unkind brow.
And dart not scornful glances from those eyes
A woman moved is like a fountain troubled,
Muddy, ill seeming... thick, bereft of beauty.
SCIENCE OFFICER. Come come, you froward and unable
worm.
My mind has been as big as one of yours
My heart as great, my IQ haply more.
TEMPEST. Take thy face hence woman, I am sick at heart.
SCIENCE OFFICER. Misogony is sickness of the mind.
TEMPEST. Mind sickness, and where did you read that?
SCIENCE OFFICER. 'Tis physic sir, as taught by Sigmund
Freud.
TEMPEST. Throw physic to the dogs, I'll none of it.
This is a man's world

SCIENCE OFFICER. *(Sings.)*
BUT IT WOULDN'T BE NOTHING
WITHOUT A WOMAN ON EARTH.
TEMPEST.
YOU SEE, MAN MADE THE CAR
TO TAKE US OVER THE ROAD
MAN MADE THE TRAIN
TO CARRY THE HEAVY LOAD
MAN MADE THE ELECTRIC LIGHT
TO TAKE US OUT OF THE DARK
MAN MADE THE BOAT FOR THE WATER LIKE...
SCIENCE OFFICER.
NOAH MADE THE ARK?
TEMPEST.
THIS IS A MAN'S WORLD.
SCIENCE OFFICER.
BUT IT WOULDN'T BE NOTHING
WITHOUT A WOMAN ON EARTH.

(Spoken. Music vamps under.)

    You have some sick offense within your mind
    Which by the rights and virtue of my rank
    I ought to know of.
    TEMPEST. Prithee hold thy tongue.
    SCIENCE OFFICER. *(Sings.)*
TELL ME, WHO MAKES THE LITTLE BITTY BABY GIRL
AND THE BABY BOY?
    TEMPEST.
BUT MAN MAKES THEM HAPPY
'COS MAN MAKES THEM TOYS.
    SCIENCE OFFICER.
AND HOW CAN MAN MAKE EVERYTHING
EVERYTHING HE CAN?
    TEMPEST.
'COS MAN MAKES THE MONEY
TO BUY FROM OTHER MEN.
THIS IS A MAN'S WORLD.
    SCIENCE OFFICER.
BUT IT WOULDN'T BE NOTHING
WITHOUT A WOMAN ON EARTH.

(The song is interrupted as panic breaks out on the flight deck.)

    NAVIGATIONAL OFFICER. Our sensors, sir, are picking up a
storm
    Of asteroids approaching very fast.
    SCIENCE OFFICER. Evasive action should be taken now,
    Or else we'll hit them.
    BOSUN. Look out!

*(Whizzing noise as an asteroid passes over the spaceship, followed
    by an explosion.)*

    BOSUN.   Holy cow!
They shake my nerves and they rattle my brain!
    SCIENCE OFFICER. These asteroids would drive a man insane.

(Explosion.)

> **TEMPEST**. Damage report. Damage report
> **CREW MEMBERS.** They've broke the shield!

(Explosion.)

> We'll all be killed!

(Explosion.)

> **TEMPEST.** Goodness gracious, great balls of fire!

(On the video screen we see an asteroid storm. "Great Balls of Fire" plays as an instrumental under the following.)

> **TEMPEST.** Bosun.
> **BOSUN.** Here master. What cheer?
> **TEMPEST**. Fall to it smartly, prepare the Photon Shields
> Or else our cause is lost. Bestir, bestir!
> **OMNES.** *(Sing.)*
GOODNESS GRACIOUS, GREAT BALLS OF FIRE!
> **TEMPEST.** *(Spoken.)* Hey my hearts,
> Cheerly cheerly my hearts,
> Quick, quick, put up the force field—
> **BOSUN.** Tend to the Captain's orders.
> **SCIENCE OFFICER.** Good Captain have care. Let's us the
shuttlecraft.
> Play the men.
> **TEMPEST.** I pray you keep below.

(She doesn't move.)

> **BOSUN.** Do you not hear him? You mar our labor.
> **TEMPEST.** Keep your cabin. You do assist the storm!
> **COOKIE.** *(Sings.)*
I CHEW MY NAILS AND I TWIDDLE MY THUMBS,
I'M REALLY NERVOUS AND THIS AIN'T NO FUN.

SCIENCE OFFICER. *(Spoken.)* Come back baby, I'm going crazy!

OMNES. *(Sing.)*

GOODNESS GRACIOUS, GREAT BALLS OF FIRE!

TEMPEST. *(Spoken.)* Down with the Warpspeed. Quickly, lower, lower.

Bring her to try with main course.

SCIENCE OFFICER.   But Captain...

TEMPEST. A plague upon this howling; you are louder

Than the weather, or our office.

SCIENCE OFFICER. A pox on your throat! You bawling blasphemous

Uncharitable dog.

TEMPEST. Lay her ahold. Set her two courses into

Space again. Lay her off.

SCIENCE OFFICER. All lost, to prayers, to prayers, all lost!

COOKIE. Mercy on us, we split, we split.

BOSUN. Farewell, my wife and children. Farewell, brother.

COOKIE. We split, we split.

OMNES. *(Sing.)*

GOODNESS GRACIOUS, GREAT BALLS OF FIRE!

BOSUN. Now would I give a thousand light years of space

For an acre of barren ground.

SCIENCE OFFICER. The wills above be done.

But I would fain die a terrestrial death.

(Sings.)

HELP ME BABY.

TEMPEST.

I DON'T FEEL SO GOOD.

BOSUN.

HOLD IT LADY—HEY

PLEASE TRY TO ACT LIKE A DOCTOR SHOULD.

(The SCIENCE OFFICER exits.)

TEMPEST. I must confess, we're in a mess!

NAVIGATIONAL OFFICER. *(Sings.)*

CAN YOU HEAR US EARTH? THIS IS AN SOS.

OMNES. Yes! *(Sing.)*
I CHEW MY NAILS AND I TWIDDLE MY THUMBS,
I'M REALLY NERVOUS AND THIS AIN'T NO FUN.
  BOSUN.
COME BACK BABY, S'DRIVING ME CRAZY!
  OMNES. *(Sing.)*
GOODNESS GRACIOUS GREAT BALLS OF...

(The song finishes abruptly. Eerie music is heard. Throughout the following scene, we see a gradual descent from space to the surface of a planet on the video screen.)

  TEMPEST. Where should this music be?
The air or the Earth?
  NAVIGATIONAL OFFICER. It sounds no more, but sure it waits
Upon some force on yonder planet.
This music creeps by us through the asteroids
Allaying both their fury and my passion
With its sweet air.
  TEMPEST. Thence have we followed it
Or it has drawn us rather,
(The eerie music stops.)
  But it's gone.

(The music begins again.)

  BOSUN. No, it begins again.
  NAVIGATIONAL OFFICER. We have been caught within a
tractor beam
Which seems to emanate from yonder star.
  BOSUN. The Chief says that we cannot pull away,
There seems to be nothing that he can do.
  TEMPEST. Quick, get the Science Officer aloft.
I need advice. I haven't got a plan.
  BOSUN. She's gone sir, taking our last shuttlecraft.
(A shuttlecraft flies over the ship.)
And now is just a blip upon our screen.
  TEMPEST. It's court martial if ever she is found.

BOSUN. But sir I can't believe it's cowardice.
TEMPEST. Speak not you for her. She's a traitor...

(The space ship crash-lands with a crash and a dipping of lights. The music stops.)

BOSUN.   Cripes.
TEMPEST. What planet, friend, is this?

(The NAVIGATIONAL OFFICER checks the controls.)

NAVIGATIONAL OFFICER. D'Illyria, Captain.
TEMPEST. And what should I do on D'Illyria?
BOSUN. I think we're gonna need the valium.
NAVIGATIONAL OFFICER.
This planet has a pleasant seat: the air
Nimbly and sweetly recommends itself
Unto our probing sensors and I see
They have observed the air is delicate.
TEMPEST. But why were we caught in a tractor beam?
BOSUN. D'Illyria is not marked upon our charts.
NAVIGATIONAL OFFICER. There seems to be a signal coming through
Upon our scanner screen.

(Synthesizer effect.)

BOSUN. Then patch us in.
TEMPEST. All torment, trouble, wonder and amazement
Inhabits here. Some alien power holds us
On this fearful planet.
NAVIGATIONAL OFFICER. Behold Captain!

(PROSPERO appears on the video screen.)

TEMPEST. My God, I know that face. It's Prospero
Who fifteen years ago, this very day,
Defected to the other side, they say.

PROSPERO. Not so my friends, but please collect yourselves.
No more amazement. Tell your piteous hearts
There's no harm done.
TEMPEST.   You'll rue this day.
PROSPERO.   No harm.
I have done nothing but in care of thee;
Of thee and my dear one, my daughter, who
Is ignorant of what I am, naught knowing
Of whence I came nor that I am more better
Than Prospero, master of a full poor lab,
And her no greater father.

(PROSPERO sings, "Don't Let Me Be Misunderstood".)

 PROSPERO.
HEY MAN, DO YOU UNDERSTAND ME NOW
IF SOMETIMES I FEEL A LITTLE MAD?
BUT DON'T YOU KNOW THAT NO ONE ALIVE CAN
 ALWAYS BE AN ANGEL?
WHEN THINGS GO WRONG I SEEM TO BE BAD.
BUT I'M JUST A SOUL WHOSE INTENTIONS ARE GOOD.
OH LORD, PLEASE DON'T LET ME BE MISUNDERSTOOD.

(Spoken. Music vamps under.)

 TEMPEST. Quit stalling Prospero, and tell us straight
For what vile scheme you brought us here.
PROSPERO.   'Tis time
I should inform thee further, lend an ear.
(On the video screen a black and white "B" movie flashback appears.
 It shows the events which PROSPERO relates.)
My wife and lab assistant Gloria,
I pray you mark me—that a mother should
Be so perfidious—she whom next my child
Of all the world I loved and to her put
The manage of my lab, as at that time
Through all the subsidies it was the first
And Prospero the tops, being so reputed

In dignity and scientific arts without a parallel:
These being all my study, the government had set me on a
project
And I had nearly cracked it, being transported
And rapt in secret studies. Then my wife,
Dost thou attend me?
TEMPEST.   Sir, most heedfully.
PROSPERO. I thus neglected worldly ends, all dedicate
To closeness and the bettering of my mind.
I cannot tell what happened to my wife
But something evil grew within her breast
And just as we the project did complete
She stuck me up and bound me hands and feet.
TEMPEST. Wherefore did she not that hour destroy you?

(The film pauses and PROSPERO re-appears on the screen.)

PROSPERO. Well demanded sir.
My tale provokes that question. Sir, she dare not.
(The film continues.)
In few, she hurried me aboard a craft,
A rotten carcass of a satellite,
With very little chance I should survive
And launched this spaceship through the Galaxy.
But in this ship my baby daughter slept.
Because of savings I had tried to fight
The lab had axed its créche facility.
This was the most unkindest cut of all.

(The film finishes and PROSPERO re-appears on the screen.)

TEMPEST. A tragic tale and most inglorious fall.
PROSPERO. *(Sings.)*
IF I SEEM EDGY I WANT YOU TO KNOW
THAT I NEVER MEAN TO TAKE IT OUT ON YOU
LIFE HAS IT'S PROBLEMS AND I'VE GOT MY SHARE
BUT THERE'S ONE THING I NEVER MEAN TO DO
OH NO...

(Spoken—music vamps under.)
    Hey man,
    Don't you know I'm human,
    Have thoughts like any other one?
    Sometime I find myself
    Long long regretting
    Some foolish thing
    Some little simple thing I've said or done.
(Sings.)
I'M JUST A SOUL WHOSE INTENTIONS ARE GOOD.
OH LORD, PLEASE DON'T LET ME BE MISUNDERSTOOD
YES, I'M JUST A SOUL WHOSE INTENTIONS ARE GOOD.
OH LORD, PLEASE DON'T LET ME BE MISUNDERSTOOD.
    TEMPEST. Oh never was a story of more woe
    Than this of Gloria and her Prospero.
    PROSPERO. At last, though long, you've come to rescue me
    And, though I had to bring your ship down sir,
    Let's smile at scapes and perils overblown.
    Please, honored Captain, I do bid you welcome.
    TEMPEST. While I with selfsame kindness welcome you.
(PROSPERO disappears from the video screen.)
    Feast with the best and welcome to my ship.
    We'll banquet now, to close our stomachs up
    After initial fears.
(PROSPERO enters through the air-lock. COOKIE uses the micro-
    phone as a Geiger counter to check him.)
    Pray you come in.
    For now we meet to chat as well as eat.
    COOKIE. Nothing but sit in ship and eat and eat.
(ARIEL the robot enters through the air-lock to the opening bars of
    "Thus Spracht Zarathrustra". Lights dip.)
    Avaunt and quit my sight, let the earth hide thee.
    Thy bones are marrowless, they blood is cold.
    Thou hast no speculation in those eyes
    Which thou dost glare with.
    PROSPERO. Think of this friends but as a thing of metal,
    'Tis no other.
    COOKIE. Well it ain't human, sir. It frightens me.

PROSPERO. But he is friendly. He does make our fire,
Fetch in our wood, and serves in offices
That profit us. His name is Ariel.
*(COOKIE uses the microphone as a Geiger counter to check the ro-
bot. It goes haywire and drags COOKIE towards ARIEL. COOKIE
gets a terrific electric shock and is thrown to the floor.)*
Now Robot speak.
ARIEL. There's wood enough within.
Hi, cats. My name is Ariel. Beep! Beep!
I am the invention of the Doctor who
Took pains to make me speak, taught me each hour
One thing or other when I did'st not
Know mine own meaning, but would
Gabble like a thing most brutish.
TEMPEST. You are most welcome.
Good Doctor Prospero, before we leave
We have a problem.
ARIEL.   Yes, of this we know.
You need to find your Science Officer
Who fled your spaceship in its hour of need.
I tracked her on my radar screen until
She dipped below the horizon, and then
Upon the planet's dark side vanished.
PROSPERO. Now Ariel, emit a scanner ray.
I'll know the fate of this lost shuttlecraft,
Its disposition and position.

*(ARIEL starts to scan to the opening bars of "Good Vibrations".
MIRANDA enters through the air-lock.)*

COOKIE. Wow!
TEMPEST. But soft. What light from yonder air-lock breaks?
PROSPERO. It is my daughter.
COOKIE.   Jeepers, what a 'hon!
TEMPEST. *(Sings.)*
I, I LOVE THE COLORFUL CLOTHES SHE WEARS
AND THE WAY THE SUNLIGHT PLAYS UPON HER HAIR.
I HEAR THE SOUND OF HER GENTLE WORD

ON THE WIND THAT LIFTS HER PERFUME THROUGH THE
   AIR.

(ARIEL spins as if scanning the horizon.)

   ARIEL. *(Sings.)*
I'M PICKING UP GOOD VIBRATIONS
SHE'S GIVING ME EXCITATIONS
I'M PICKING UP GOOD VIBRATIONS
SHE'S GIVING ME EXCITATIONS
I'M PICKING UP GOOD VIBRATIONS
SHE'S GIVING ME EXCITATIONS
I'M PICKING UP GOOD VIBRATIONS
SHE'S GIVING ME EXCITATIONS
   TEMPEST.
CLOSE MY EYES, SHE'S SOMEHOW CLOSER NOW
SOFTLY SMILE I KNOW SHE MUST BE KIND.
WHEN I LOOK IN HER EYES
SHE COMES WITH ME TO A BLOSSOM WORLD.
   ARIEL.
I'M PICKING UP GOOD VIBRATIONS
SHE'S GIVING ME EXCITATIONS
I'M PICKING UP GOOD VIBRATIONS
SHE'S GIVING ME EXCITATIONS
I'M PICKING UP GOOD VIBRATIONS
SHE'S GIVING ME EXCITATIONS
   TEMPEST/PROSPERO.
GOOD GOOD GOOD GOOD VIBRATIONS AAAAA
GOOD GOOD GOOD GOOD VIBRATIONS AAAAA
GOOD GOOD GOOD GOOD VIBRATIONS AAAAA
   PROSPERO. *(Spoken—music vamps under.)* Go Robot, go and
find this shuttlecraft.
   There are yet missing of this company.
   Go search it out and bring it hither straight.
   ARIEL. *(Sings.)*
I DON'T KNOW WHERE BUT HE SENDS ME THERE.

(ARIEL exits.)

CREW.
MY MY MY WHAT A SENSATION
MY MY MY WHAT ELATION
MY MY MY WHAT A...
   TEMPEST.
GOT TO KEEP THOSE LOVING GOOD VIBRATIONS
HAPPENING WITH HER
   TEMPEST AND CREW.
GOT TO KEEP THOSE LOVING GOOD VIBRATIONS
HAPPENING WITH HER
GOT TO KEEP THOSE LOVING GOOD VIBRATIONS
HAPPENING WITH HER
GOT TO KEEP THOSE LOVING GOOD VIBRATIONS
HAPPENING WITH HER

(Spoken—music vamps under.)

   PROSPERO. Captain, may I present my little girl.
Miranda, say hello.
   MIRANDA. What, is't a spirit?
   PROSPERO. No wench, it eats and sleeps and hath
Such senses as we have such.
   MIRANDA. I might call him divine,
For nothing natural could be so fair.

(MIRANDA and TEMPEST touch.)

   OMNES. (Sing.)
AH!
GOOD, GOOD, GOOD, GOOD VIBRATIONS
SHE'S GIVING ME EXCITATIONS
GOOD, GOOD, GOOD, GOOD VIBRATIONS
I'M PICKING UP GOOD VIBRATIONS
SHE'S GIVING ME EXCITATIONS
I'M PICKING UP EXCITATIONS
NA NA NA NA NA NA NA NA
NA NA NA NA NA NA NA NA
GOOD GOOD GOOD GOOD VIBRATIONS

TEMPEST. Excuse me Ma'am.
PROSPERO. Good Captain list, a word.

(PROSPERO takes TEMPEST aside.)

COOKIE. Oh she doth teach the torches to burn bright
It seems she hangs upon the cheek of night
Like a rich jewel in an Ethiop's ear
Did my heart live 'til now, forswear it sight
For I ne'er saw true beauty 'til tonight.
BOSUN. Hey Cookie tell me is it possible
That love should of a sudden take such hold?
COOKIE. Oh sir, until I found it to be true
I never thought it possible or likely.
But see, while idly I stood looking on,
I found the effect of love in idleness.
BOSUN. Cookie you looked so longly on the dame
Perhaps you marked not what's the pith of all.
COOKIE. Oh sir, I saw her coral lips to move
And with her breath she did perfume the air
Sacred and sweet was all I saw in her
BOSUN. Oh come on Cookie, snap out of this trance,
I pray awake boy: if you do love this chick
Bend thoughts and wits to achieve her.
COOKIE. Oh sir, I burn, I pine, I perish Bosun,
If I achieve not this young modest girl.
Counsel me Bosun for I know thou can'st
Assist me Bosun for I know thou wilt.

(COOKIE sings "The Shoop Shoop Song".)

COOKIE. *(Sings.)*
DOES SHE LOVE ME I WANNA KNOW
HOW CAN I TELL IF SHE LOVES ME SO?
IS IT IN HER EYES?
BOSUN.
OH, NO YOU'LL BE DECEIVED

COOKIE.
IS IT IN HER EYES?
BOSUN.
OH, NO YOU'LL MAKE BELIEVE
IF YOU WANNA KNOW
IF SHE LOVES YOU SO
IT'S IN HER KISS
COOKIE.
IS IT IN HER FACE?
BOSUN.
OH, NO THAT'S JUST HER CHARM
COOKIE.
IN HER WARM EMBRACE?

(COOKIE grabs the BOSUN.)

BOSUN.
OH, NO THAT'S JUST MY ARM
IF YOU WANNA KNOW
IF SHE LOVES YOU SO
IT'S IN HER KISS

OH, HUG HER KISS HER
AND SQUEEZE HER TIGHT
AND FIND OUT WHAT
YOU WANNA KNOW
IF IT'S LOVE,
YES, IF IT REALLY IS
IT'S THERE IN HER KISS
COOKIE.
ABOUT THE WAY SHE ACTS
BOSUN.
OH NO THAT'S NOT THE WAY
AND YOU'RE NOT LISTENING
TO ALL I SAY
IF YOU WANNA KNOW
IF SHE LOVES YOU SO
IT'S IN HER KISS
THAT'S WHERE IT IS.

COOKIE.
OH, YEAH IT'S IN HER KISS
(The following exchange is spoken—music vamps under.)
   Sweet Lady
   MIRANDA. Hi, what say'st thou, Cookie?
   COOKIE. Sweet Lady, pity me.
   MIRANDA. Why I am sorry for thee gentle friend.
   COOKIE. Wherever sorry is relief would be
If you do sorrow at my grief in love
By giving love, your sorrow and my grief
Were both extermin'd.
   MIRANDA. Thou hast my love. *(She kisses COOKIE on the cheek.)*   Is that not neighborly?
   COOKIE. Her lips suck forth my soul. See where it flies!
   BOSUN. *(Sings.)*
OH, HUG HER, KISS HER
AND SQUEEZE HER TIGHT
AND FIND OUT WHAT
YOU WANNA KNOW
IF IT'S LOVE,
   COOKIE.
YES IT REALLY IS
   BOSUN.
IT'S THERE IN HER KISS
ABOUT THE WAY SHE ACTS
   COOKIE.
OH NO THAT'S NOT THE WAY
AND YOU'RE NOT LISTENING
TO ALL I SAY
IF YOU WANNA KNOW
WHY SHE LOVES ME SO
IT'S IN HER KISS
THAT'S WHERE IT IS
   BOSUN/COOKIE.
THAT'S WHERE IT IS!

(ARIEL enters.)

ARIEL. Bosun, Bosun, good news and bad news as
You never heard of.
BOSUN. Is it good news and bad news too? How may that be?
ARIEL. Is it not good to hear your Science Officer is coming?
BOSUN. Is she come?
ARIEL. Why no sir.
BOSUN. What then?
ARIEL. She is coming.
BOSUN. When will she be here?
ARIEL. When she stands where I am and sees you there.
TEMPEST. Thou still hast been the father of good news.
ARIEL. Thank you and I assure you sir
I hold my duty as you hold your soul
Unto my God, that is my creator.
TEMPEST. But do you think, or else that brain of yours
Reads not the plans of humanoids so sure
As it has used to—that you have found
The secret of your master's discov'ry?
Oh speak of that; that do I long to hear.
ARIEL. Certainly sir, I worked on it myself.
And since I am not programmed for deceit
I will relate my master's great break-through
Which once it has but stabilized itself
Will rank him with the greatest men of yore.
Copernicus, Darwin, yeah e'en Einstein.
TEMPEST. He tells us Bosun that he hath found out
The head and source of Prospero's great find.
BOSUN. Well?
TEMPEST. I shall sift him.

*(Introduction to "I'm Gonna Change the World" vamps under the
    following.)*

ARIEL. My Master, bless the hands that made my parts,
Had worked for many years in solitude
Upon a revolution'ry idea
A form of science 'Telegenesis'.

(Guitar chord.)

TEMPEST. Telegenesis?
ARIEL. Which is creation by pure thought alone
Without need of instrumentality.
BOSUN. But that's..... impossible.
ARIEL. Creation of pure matter with the mind.
To make this work and here I use lay terms,
One must open nine-tenths of the brain
Which ordinary mortals never use,
It's called "cerebral elasticity".

(Guitar chord.)

TEMPEST & BOSUN. Cerebral elasticity?
ARIEL. The break-through came when Doctor Prospero
Distilled a drug he called the "X Factor"
Which utilized this untapped grey matter.
He took a draught, while in the lab one day,
And hasn't been himself, I'm sad to say.
PROSPERO. My robot seems t'have run off at the mouth.
This walking Coke-can better watch its step
Or I'll be forced to take his spark plugs out.
TEMPEST. *(Sings.)*
HOLD YOUR FIRE! NOW, LISTEN MISTER
DON'T CAUSE NO TROUBLE FOR MY BROTHER OR SISTER.
WHY DON'T YOU LOOK ME IN THE FACE?
EITHER THAT OR LEAVE MY PLACE.
    ARIEL.
HE'S GONNA CHANGE THE WORLD
HE'S GONNA CHANGE THE WORLD
HE'LL SWITCH YOUR WRONG TO RIGHT
YOU CAN BET YOUR LIFE.
    PROSPERO.
THERE'S ONE THING I GOTTA SAY
THERE'S GOT TO BE SOME CHANGES MADE
NO MORE BLACK NO MORE WHITE
NO MORE WRONG NO MORE RIGHT

'CAUSE I'M GONNA CHANGE THE WORLD
I'M GONNA CHANGE THE WORLD
I'LL SWITCH YOUR WRONG TO RIGHT
YOU CAN BET YOUR LIFE.
YES, I'M GONNA CHANGE THE WORLD
I'M GONNA CHANGE THE WORLD
I'LL SWITCH YOUR WRONG TO RIGHT
YOU CAN BET YOUR LIFE.

(Spoken—music vamps under.)

MIRANDA. Why speaks my father so ungently?
This is the third man that e'er I saw, the first
That e'er I sighed for; pity move my father
To be inclined my way.
PROSPERO. Silence my child! *(To TEMPEST.)*
One more word I charge thee.
 Thou dost usurp the name thou ow'st not; and has put thyself
Upon this planet as a spy to steal my formula.
ARIEL. No, as he is a man!
PROSPERO. I would not be surprised if thou were not
In league with Gloria my evil spouse.
MIRANDA. There's nothing ill can dwell in such a temple.
If the ill spirit have so fair a house,
Good things will strive to dwell within it.
PROSPERO. But goes thy heart with this?
MIRANDA. Aye my good lord.
PROSPERO. So young and so untender.
MIRANDA. So young my lord and true.
PROSPERO. Let it be so, thy truth then be thy dower.
Here I disclaim all my paternal care,
Propinquity and property of blood
And as a stranger to my heart and me
Hold thee from this forever.
OMNES. Golly gee!

(MIRANDA sings to TEMPEST "A Teenager in Love?")

MIRANDA. *(Spoken to PROSPERO.)* Each time we have a quarrel
It almost breaks my heart
'Cos I'm so afraid
That we will have to part
Each night I ask the stars up above

(MIRANDA sings to TEMPEST.)

MIRANDA.
WHY MUST I BE A TEENAGER IN LOVE?
(To PROSPERO.)
ONE DAY I FEEL SO HAPPY
NEXT DAY I FEEL SO SAD
I GUESS I'LL HAVE TO TAKE
THE GOOD WITH THE BAD
EACH NIGHT I ASK THE STARS UP ABOVE
(To TEMPEST.)
WHY MUST I BE A TEENAGER IN LOVE?

(Seething with anger, PROSPERO exits.)

(To PROSPERO.)
I CRIED A TEAR
FOR NOBODY BUT YOU
I'LL BE THE LONELY ONE
IF YOU SHOULD SAY WE'RE THROUGH

(COOKIE enters and thinks that MIRANDA is singing the song for him.)

SO IF YOU WANT TO MAKE ME CRY
THAT WON'T BE SO HARD TO DO
AND IF YOU SHOULD SAY GOODBYE
I'LL STILL GO ON LOVING YOU
EACH NIGHT I ASK THE STARS UP ABOVE
WHY MUST I BE A TEENAGER IN LOVE?
WHY MUST I BE A TEENAGER IN LOVE?

WHY MUST I BE A TEENAGER IN LOVE?
WHY MUST I BE A TEENAGER IN LOVE?
   OMNES.
IN LOVE.
   MIRANDA. I love you father, but my heart is here.
Turn back dull earth and find thy centre out.
(To COOKIE.)
   Thou know'st the mask of night is on my face
Else would a maiden blush bepaint my cheek.
For that which thou has heard me speak tonight
Fain would I dwell on form, fain fain deny
What I have spoke: but farewell compliment!
(To TEMPEST.)
   Dost thou love me? I know thou wilt say
And I will take thy word.

(COOKIE exits, heartbroken.)

   TEMPEST. Now look here child,
By innocence I swear and by your youth
I have one heart, one bosom and one truth
And that no woman has, nor never none
Shall master be of it, save I alone.

(TEMPEST sings "Young Girl".)

   TEMPEST.
YOUNG GIRL GET OUT OF MY MIND
MY LOVE FOR YOU IS WAY OUT OF LINE
BETTER RUN GIRL
YOU'RE MUCH TOO YOUNG GIRL

WITH ALL THE CHARMS OF A WOMAN
YOU'VE KEPT THE SECRET OF YOUR YOUTH
YOU LED ME TO BELIEVE, YOU'RE OLD ENOUGH
TO GIVE ME LOVE
AND NOW IT HURTS TO KNOW THE TRUTH.

YOUNG GIRL GET OUT OF MY MIND
MY LOVE FOR YOU IS WAY OUT OF LINE
BETTER RUN GIRL
YOU'RE MUCH TOO YOUNG GIRL

WITHOUT THE PERFUME AND MAKE-UP
YOU'RE JUST A BABY IN DISGUISE
AND ALTHOUGH YOU KNOW, IT'S WRONG TO BE
IN LOVE WITH ME
THAT COME ON LOOKS IN YOUR EYES

YOUNG GIRL GET OUT OF MY MIND
MY LOVE FOR YOU IS WAY OUT OF LINE
BETTER RUN GIRL
YOU'RE MUCH TOO YOUNG GIRL

(Instrumental.)

SO HURRY HOME TO YOUR PAPA
I'M SURE HE WONDERS WHERE YOU ARE
GET OUT OF HERE BEFORE I HAVE THE TIME
TO CHANGE MY MIND
BECAUSE I'M AFRAID WE'LL GO TOO FAR
   OMNES.
YOUNG GIRL GET OUT OF MY MIND
MY LOVE FOR YOU IS WAY OUT OF LINE
BETTER RUN GIRL
   TEMPEST.
YOU'RE MUCH TOO YOUNG GIRL

(Spoken)

And so adieu young lady, don't be sad
But can't you see that you've upset your dad?
MIRANDA. Oh what a deal of scorn looks beautiful
In the contempt and anger of his lip.
A murderous guilt shows not itself more soon
Than love that would seem hid, loves' night is noon,

Oh, Captain, by the roses of the spring
By maidhood, honor, truth and everything
I love thee so that despite all your pride
Nor wit nor reason can my passion hide.
(Sings.)
WHY MUST I BE A TEENAGER IN LOVE?
  COOKIE. *(Sings.)*
WHY MUST I BE A TEENAGER IN LOVE?
  (Spoken.) Is there no pity sitting in the clouds
  That sees into the bottom of my grief?
  You kissed my cheek, I thought you favored me
  But you professed your love to the Captain.
(MIRANDA exits.)
  Oh Miranda this love that thou hast shown
  Doth add more grief to too much of mine own,
  Love is a smoke raised with the fume of sighs,
  Being purged, a fire sparkling in lover's eyes;
  Being vexed, a sea nourished with lover's tears.
(The CREW laugh.)
  They laugh at me, the Captain and the crew.
  I'll be revenged on the whole pack of you!

(COOKIE sings "She's Not There".)

  COOKIE.
WELL NO ONE TOLD ME ABOUT HER
THE WAY SHE LIED
WELL NO ONE TOLD ME ABOUT HER
HOW MANY PEOPLE CRIED
BUT IT'S TOO LATE TO SAY YOU'RE SORRY
HOW COULD I KNOW, WHY SHOULD I CARE
WELL PLEASE DON'T BOTHER TRYING TO FIND HER
SHE'S NOT THERE.

WELL LET ME TELL YOU 'BOUT THE WAY SHE LOOKS
THE WAY SHE ACTS AND THE COLOR OF HER HAIR
HER VOICE WAS SOFT AND COOL
HER EYES WERE CLEAR AND BRIGHT

BUT SHE'S NOT THERE

WELL NO ONE TOLE ME ABOUT HER
WHAT COULD I DO?
WELL NO ONE TOLD ME ABOUT HER
THOUGH THEY ALL KNEW
BUT IT'S TOO LATE TO SAY YOU'RE SORRY
HOW COULD I KNOW, WHY SHOULD I CARE?
WELL PLEASE DON'T BOTHER TRYING TO FIND HER
SHE'S NOT THERE.

WELL LET ME TELL YOU 'BOUT THE WAY SHE LOOKS
THE WAY SHE ACTS AND THE COLOR OF HER HAIR
HER VOICE WAS SOFT AND COOL
HER EYES WERE CLEAR AND BRIGHT
BUT SHE'S NOT THERE

(Spoken—music vamps under.)

    Thou nature art my goodness; to they law
    My services are bound. Wherefore should I
    Stand in the plague of custom and permit
    The Captain of this spaceship to deprive me
    When my dimensions are as well compact,
    My mind as generous, my shape as true
    As is the issue of this Tempest's mum?

(Sings.)

WELL LET ME TELL YOU 'BOUT THE WAY SHE LOOKS
THE WAY SHE ACTS AND THE COLOR OF HER HAIR
HER VOICE WAS SOFT AND COOL
HER EYES WERE CLEAR AND BRIGHT
BUT SHE'S NOT THERE.

*(COOKIE plays a guitar solo, which should reflect his inner tur-
    moil.)*

WELL LET ME TELL YOU 'BOUT THE WAY SHE LOOKED
THE WAY SHE ACTS AND THE COLOR OF HER HAIR
HER VOICE WAS SOFT AND COOL
HER EYES WERE CLEAR AND BRIGHT
BUT SHE'S NOT THERE.

(Spoken—music vamps under.)

    Well my fancy Captain, if I get the chance
    And I can find a way, Cookie the base
    Shall top this Tempest. I grow, I prosper.
    Now God stand up for bastards!
(Sings.)
'COS SHE'S NOT THERE!

(BLACKOUT.)

(The lights come up. PROSPERO enters.)

    PROSPERO. I never felt a passion so confused,
    So strange, outrageous or so variable.
    My daughter, oh my child, my daughter,
    Fled with the Captain, oh that vile space wolf.
*(The introduction to "Shaking All Over" begins and vamps under the
    following. The effect of this scene should be that PROSPERO is
    alone and that MIRANDA and TEMPEST are merely images in
    his mind.)*
    Blow winds and crack your cheeks! Rage! Blow!
    You cataracts and hurricanoes spout
    Till you have drenched our steeples,
    drowned the cocks!
    You sulph'rous and thought-executing fires,
    Strike flat and thick rotundity of this world!
    Crack nature's moulds, all germens spill at once
    That makes ingrateful man!
    I am a dad more sinned against than sinning.
    Well bless my soul what's wrong with me?
    I'm itching like a man on amphetamine.

My child says I'm acting wild as a six legged segmented inverte-brate.

(A spot comes up on MIRANDA.)

MIRANDA. (Sings.)
I'M IN LOVE!

(A spot comes up on TEMPEST.)

TEMPEST.
I'M SHAKING ALL OVER.
WHEN SHE MOVES UP RIGHT UP CLOSE TO ME
THAT'S WHEN I GET THE SHAKES ALL OVER ME
   MIRANDA.
QUIVERS DOWN MY BACK BONE.
   TEMPEST.
I GOT THE SHAKES IN MY KNEE BONE.
   MIRANDA.
SHIVERS DOWN MY THIGH BONE
   PROSPERO.
I'M SHAKING ALL OVER.

(Spoken—music vamps under.)

Thou has her Tempest. Let her be thine, for we
Have no such daughter. Nor shall ever see
That face of hers again—therefore, begone.
I loved her most and thought to set my rest
On her kind nursery—hence and avoid my sight.
(Lights out on TEMPEST and MIRANDA.)
Come cordial sweet, come puissant "X Factor"
The panacea for my fevered brain.
(PROSPERO drinks from a test tube marked "X Factor".)
Oh true apothecary! Thy drug is quick!
(Sings.)
QUIVERS DOWN MY BACK BONE
I GOT THE SHAKES IN MY KNEE BONE

SHIVERS DOWN MY THIGH BONE
I'M SHAKING ALL OVER.

I GOT THE SHAKES IN MY KNEE BONE
TREMORS IN MY THIGH BONE
I'M SHAKING...
I'M SHAKING... SHAKING... SHAKING
ALL OVER

(PROSPERO collapses. Blackout. During the Blackout the introduction to "Gloria" begins. the lights come up and the music builds slowly during the following scene.)

TEMPEST. Look to the Doctor.
BOSUN.   Sir, are you OK?
PROSPERO. Do not muse at me, my worthy friend.
I have a strange infirmity which is
Nothing to those who know me.
NAVIGATIONAL OFFICER. Captain! Captain!
TEMPEST. Who calls so loud?
NAVIGATIONAL OFFICER. There is a beep upon my scanner
screen.
ARIEL. That is no doubt your Science Officer.
BOSUN. Convey her, Ariel, as you were charged.
NAVIGATIONAL OFFICER. But hold. I think I have another
beep.
TEMPEST. A second beep?
NAVIGATIONAL OFFICER. Well I'm not really sure.
TEMPEST. Two beeps, or not two beeps.
NAVIGATIONAL OFFICER.   That is the question
The second's larger, monstrous in shape
And travels with most unwarrantable speed
Towards this spaceship, chasing her I think.
TEMPEST. Angels and ministers of grace defend us.
Is this a spirit of health or goblin damn'd?
Be its intents wicked or charitable?
It com'st in such a questionable shape.

PROSPERO. There are more things in Heaven and Earth
Than are dreamt of in my laboratory.
NAVIGATIONAL OFFICER. A score of years and ten I can
remember well
Within the volume of which time I have see
Hours dreadful and things strange, but this sore sight
Hath trifled former knowings.
BOSUN. Then patch us in!

(A monster appears on the video screen.)

COOKIE. Is this a monster that I see before me
With tentacles instead of hands. Don't let it clutch me!
PROSPERO. I see it not!
TEMPEST. And yet I see it still!
PROSPERO. Are thou not, fatal vision, sensible
To me as to his sight, or art thou but
A monster of the mind, a false creation
Proceeding from the heat oppressed brain?
TEMPEST. Put up the force-field, that will hold it back!
NAVIGATIONAL OFFICER. Ariel and the Science Officer
Are in the air-lock, sir.
TEMPEST. Then open it!
NAVIGATIONAL OFFICER . *(Sings.)*
HERE THEY COME.
HERE THEY COME.
HERE THEY COME.
OMNES.
COMING UP THE STAIRS.
NAVIGATIONAL OFFICER.
HERE THEY COME.
OMNES.
COMING THROUGH THE FLOOR
NAVIGATIONAL OFFICER.
HERE THEY COME.

(The air-lock opens and ARIEL enters carrying the SCIENCE OF-
    FICER.)

PROSPERO. It's her, it's... GLORIA!
SCIENCE OFFICER. *(Sings.)*
AI AI AI AI AI AI!
OMNES.
GLORIA
SCIENCE OFFICER.
G. L. O. R. I. A.
OMNES.
GLORIA.
SCIENCE OFFICER.
G. L. O. R. I. A.
OMNES.
GLORIA.
SCIENCE OFFICER.
G. L. O. R. I. A.
OMNES.
GLORIA.
*(The SCIENCE OFFICER looks towards the air-lock, which glows
with an eerie green light.)*
HERE IT COMES
HERE IT COMES
HERE IT COMES
CREW.
COMING UP THE STAIRS.
SCIENCE OFFICER.
HERE IT COMES
CREW.
COMING THROUGH THE FLOOR.
SCIENCE OFFICER.
HERE IT COMES.

AI AI AI AI AI AI

(Two giant tentacles fly in.)

PROSPERO.
NIGHTMARES, NIGHTMARES, NIGHTMARES,
NIGHTMARES, NIGHTMARES.

SCIENCE OFFICER.
G. L. O. R. I. A.
OMNES.
GLORIA.
SCIENCE OFFICER.
G. L. O. R. I. A.
OMNES.
GLORIA.
SCIENCE OFFICER.
G. L. O. R. I. A.
OMNES.
GLORIA.
SCIENCE OFFICER.
G. L. O. R. I. A.
OMNES.
GLORIA

(Blackout. The video screen comes on.)

NEWSCASTER. *(On video screen.)* Will the ship be saved from this monstrous attack?
Will the Captain return Miranda's love?
Will Prospero forgive his evil wife?
Will you manage to get to the john before anyone else?
Find out this and more in the second half of,
"Return to the Forbidden Planet"!

(The lights come up showing the CREW fighting off the monster.)

SCIENCE OFFICER.
G. L. O. R. I. A.
OMNES.
GLORIA.
SCIENCE OFFICER.
G. L. O. R. I. A.
OMNES.
GLORIA.

SCIENCE OFFICER.
G. L. O. R. I. A.
   OMNES.
GLORIA.
   SCIENCE OFFICER.
G. L. O. R. I. A.
   OMNES.
GLORIA.
   SCIENCE OFFICER.
G. L. O. R. I. A.
AI AI AI AI AI AI!

(During the above one of the Monster's tentacles lifts the SCIENCE
   OFFICER (GLORIA) into the air.)

(BLACKOUT)

ACT II

OMNES. *(Sing.)*
FIVE, FOUR, THREE TWO, ONE!

NEWSCASTER. *(On video.)*
Vouchsafe to those that can't follow the story
That I may prompt them: and of such as have,
I humbly pray them to admit the excuse
Of time, of numbers and due course of things
Which cannot in their huge and proper life
Be here presented. Now lest our tale jar,
I will relate the story thus so far.
A space ship on a routine survey flight
Has been drawn to a planet by a force.
Upon it Doctor Prospero, the same
As all the world thought had defected, lives,
Working upon a mind-expanding drug.
His daughter Miranda, a beauteous girl,
Has fallen for the Captain of the ship
But he does not return her love, and worse
The spaceship's cook, a simple homespun lad,
Has got it bad for this same lovely lass.
The goodly Doctor Prospero we've learnt
Has been marooned in space for many years
Dispatched there by his mysterious wife
One Gloria, who by a strange perchance
Is Science Officer aboard this ship.
Just as this fact has been discover—red
The ship's attacked by some great monstrous shape.
Confused? Amazed? Now Gentles please take heart
For we will now commence the second part.

43

*(The video goes off. Lights up on a repeat of the final scene of ACT I.
     This time however GLORIA is saved in the nick of time by ARIEL.)*

(A monster appears on the video.)

COOKIE. Is this a monster that I see before me,
With tentacles instead of hands?
Don't let it clutch me!
PROSPERO. I see it not!
TEMPEST.   And yet I see it still!
PROSPERO. Art thou not, fatal vision, sensible
To me, as to his sight? Or art thou but
A monster of the mind, a false creation
Proceeding from the heat-oppressed brain?
TEMPEST. Put up the force field, that will hold it back.
NAVIGATIONAL OFFICER. Ariel and the Science Officer
Are in the air-lock, sir.
TEMPEST. Then open it.
NAVIGATIONAL OFFICER. *(Sings.)*
HERE THEY COME.
HERE THEY COME.
OMNES.
COMING UP THE STAIRS.
NAVIGATIONAL OFFICER.
HERE THEY COME.
OMNES.
COMING THROUGH THE FLOOR.
NAVIGATIONAL OFFICER.
HERE THEY COME.

*(The air-lock opens and ARIEL enters carrying the SCIENCE OF-
     FICER.)*

PROSPERO. It's her, its... Gloria!
SCIENCE OFFICER. *(Sings.)*
AI AI AI AI AI AI!
OMNES.
GLORIA.

SCIENCE OFFICER.
G. L. O. R. I. A.
OMNES.
GLORIA.
SCIENCE OFFICER.
G. L. O. R. I. A.
OMNES.
GLORIA.
SCIENCE OFFICER.
G. L. O. R. I. A.
OMNES.
GLORIA.

(The SCIENCE OFFICER looks toward the air-lock, which glows with an eerie green light.)

SCIENCE OFFICER.
HERE IT COMES
HERE IT COMES.
OMNES.
COMING THROUGH THE DOOR.
SCIENCE OFFICER.
HERE IT COMES.
ALL.
COMING THROUGH THE DOOR.
SCIENCE OFFICER.
HERE IT COMES
PROSPERO.
NIGHTMARES, NIGHTMARES
NIGHTMARES, NIGHTMARES, NIGHTMARES.
(Spoken—music vamps under.)
  Out damned blob, out I say!
  Once more unto the breach, dear friend, once more.
  Or close the hull up with your metal head.
  TEMPEST. Come imitate the action of the Tiger
  Stiffen the sinews.
  PROSPERO. Summon up your oil,
  TEMPEST. Disguise fair nature with hard favored rage.

(ARIEL blows fire at the monster, which explodes and vanishes. The underscore stops.)

TEMPEST. The earth has bubbles as the water has
And this was of it; wither has it vanished?

(The NAVIGATION OFFICER checks the controls.)

NAVIGATION OFFICER. Into the air and what seemed corporal
As breath into the wind. Thank God it's gone.
PROSPERO. Were such things here as we do speak about
Or have we eaten of the insane root
That takes the reason prisoner?
SCIENCE OFFICER. What e'er it was I'm sure it will return.
TEMPEST. But Doctor Prospero are you OK?
PROSPERO. I am a man again.
TEMPEST. I pray you, stand still.
BOSUN. Robot, what say'st thou?
ARIEL. My sensors registered no organism
And yet a visual scan of yonder hull
Confirmed an alien presence in the ship,
The which my phaser luckily drove off.
PROSPERO. Oh Ariel, my industrial friend, Ariel.
ARIEL. What would my potent master? Here I am.
PROSPERO. Thou and thy fearful phaser, your services
Did worthily perform and I must thank you.
BOSUN. So must we all.
TEMPEST.   Yes, and most heartily.
SCIENCE OFFICER. You have scorched the snake, not killed it.
It'll close and be itself again,
While your poor phasers remain in danger of it's former tooth.
PROSPERO. Full of scorpions is your mind, dear wife.
TEMPEST. Is this your wife, our Science Officer?
PROSPERO. This is the woman, do thy office.
TEMPEST. Gloria I arrest you at the suit of Doctor Prospero,
Your wrong—ed husband.

PROSPERO. Madam you have done me wrong, notorious wrong.
SCIENCE OFFICER. Have I Prospero? No!

("Don't Let Me Be Misunderstood" underscores the following.)

PROSPERO. Notable pirate, thou galactic thief.
What foolish boldness brought you to my mercy,
Whom thou in terms so horrid and so dear
Hast made thine enemy?
SCIENCE OFFICER. Prospero, noble sir,
Be pleased that I shake off these names you give me.
Gloria never yet was thief or pirate.
Alas, why say'st thou so?
PROSPERO. See thyself, devil!
Proper deformity shows not in the fiend
So horrid as in woman.
SCIENCE OFFICER. Oh vain fool!
Thou changed and self-covered thing, for shame,
Bemonster not thy feature.
PROSPERO. Say no more!
This woman, Captain, pray you mark my words,
Is no more than a common saboteur.
My great new science, Telegenesis,
Unlocked as 'twas by the "X Factor" drug
Could have transformed mankind, created things
By impulses from power of brain alone.
Consider friends the good it could perform:
An end to conflict, famine and disease.
TEMPEST. Oh brave new world, that could be rid of these.
PROSPERO. And she, this panacea would destroy.
TEMPEST. We shall not spend a large expense of time
Before we reckon with her several crimes.
But this is just a tempor'y reprieve
Until that time, of duty you're relieved.
SCIENCE OFFICER. *(Sings.)*
BUT I'M JUST A SOUL WHOSE INTENTIONS ARE GOOD.
OH LORD, PLEASE DON'T LET ME BE MISUNDERSTOOD.

ARIEL. I'll met by starlight, proud Glo-ri-a;
I'll manacle your feet together.
SCIENCE OFFICER. No;
I will resist such entertainment 'til
Mine enemies have more power.

(PROSPERO telegenesizes GLORIA who is forced to the floor.)

PROSPERO. Come obey!
Thy nerves are in their infancy again.
And have no vigor in them.
TEMPEST.   So they are.
ARIEL. So, who's sorry now?

(ARIEL sings "Who's Sorry Now?")

ARIEL. *(Sings.)*
WHO'S SORRY NOW?
WHO'S SORRY NOW?
WHO'S HEART IS ACHING
FOR BREAKING EACH VOW
WHO'S SAD AND BLUE
WHO'S CRYING TOO
JUST LIKE HE CRIED OVER YOU?
(Get thee to a nunnery.)
RIGHT TO THE END
JUST LIKE A FRIEND
I TRIED TO WARN YOU SOMEHOW
YOU HAD YOUR WAY
NOW YOU MUST PAY
I'M GLAD THAT YOU'RE SORRY NOW

RIGHT TO THE END
JUST LIKE A FRIEND
I TRIED TO WARN YOU SOMEHOW.
YOU HAD YOUR WAY
NOW YOU MUST PAY
I'M GLAD THAT YOU'RE SORRY

(Spoken—music vamps under.)

Sorry: Meaning: Adjective: regretful, apologetic, full of grief or sorrow, compuncious, conscience smitten, curse one's folly, lament, repent, dismal, or pining, expressing pity, pained at heart, contemptible, worthless, vile mean, poor, of little account or value. Noun: sorriness, Adverb: sorrily, comparative sorrier, Superlative: sorriest. In other words... sorry...

(Sings.)

YOU'RE SO SORRY... NOW.

TEMPEST. Look to the lady!
And when we have the spaceship's frailties fixed
That suffered in the attack, let us meet
And question this most bloody piece of work
To know it further. Fears and scruples shake us.
In the great hand of God I stand, and thence
Against the undivulged pretence I fight off
Treasonous malice.

PROSPERO. And so do I!

BOSUN. So all!

NAVIGATIONAL OFFICER. Captain Tempest, damage control report.
The spaceship's hull was fractured in the attack.

TEMPEST. Can Ariel see to it?

ARIEL.   Right away!
I'll put a girdle round the ship in twenty minutes.

(ARIEL exits.)

NAVIGATIONAL OFFICER. But that's not all. We're in another fix.

TEMPEST. Another fix? Oh no! Don't say there's more!

NAVIGATIONAL OFFICER. The Klystron Generator...

CREW.   No! Not that!

NAVIGATIONAL OFFICER. Was overloaded driving that thing off.

TEMPEST. 'Tention. Let's labor to repair the ship.
Which, monster tossed stands like a colander
Upon this planet's pitted rocky crust.

PROSPERO. The Klystron generator must be checked,
Or you will lack the power to take us hence;
And to this end, a few words, Captain pray.
BOSUN. Cookie, take her below. Lock her away.

(The crew go about their duties leaving COOKIE and the SCIENCE OFFICER alone. "She's Not There" underscores the following.)

SCIENCE OFFICER. Now is the chance to end my discontent.
Cookie, I do observe you now of late,
And have not from your eyes that gentleness
And show of love as I was wont to have.
COOKIE. Ma'am, be not deceived: I have but veiled my look.
I turn the trouble of my countenance merely upon myself.
Vexed am I of late with passions of some difference,
Which gives some soil perhaps to my behavior.
SCIENCE OFFICER. But say what sadness lengthens Cookie's hours?
COOKIE. Not having that which having shortens them.
Alas that love, so gentle in my view,
Should be so rough and tyrannous in proof.
SCIENCE OFFICER. *(Aside.)* Here's much to do with love but more with hate.
COOKIE. It is your daughter, ma'am that I do love.
I hope that you will tell me what to do;
Then would I aid you in your desperate plight.
For see, the both of us are in the wars,
And if you scratch my back I'll sure scratch yours.

(Underscore stops.)

SCIENCE OFFICER. OK Cookie, it is a deal. Let's shake.
I'll tell you how to win my daughter's love.
Now first you must obtain the formula
That Prospero developed and called "X".
If you take Prospero's great, mind expanding drug
She won't think you're a dumb cluck anymore.

COOKIE. It must be 'cause she thinks I'm dumb that she
Prefers our Captain.
SCIENCE OFFICER.   Right.
COOKIE.   Oh now I see.
SCIENCE OFFICER. And then my final hurdle I will jump
And dispatch him to an untimely grave.
COOKIE. You cannot be se-ri-ous! Take his life!
SCIENCE OFFICER. You want the meat but not the butcher's
knife.
Was the hope drunk, wherein you addressed me
And wakes it now to look so green and pale
At what it did so freely?
COOKIE.   Prithee, peace!
I dare do all that may become a man.
Who dares do more is none. I'll do the deed.

(Spot up on TEMPEST and BOSUN.)

TEMPEST. *(To BOSUN.)* Is't possible on so little acquaintance
that I
     Should like Miranda?
COOKIE. *(To SCIENCE OFFICER.)* Is't possible on so little ac-
quaintance that I
     Should like Miranda?
TEMPEST. *(To BOSUN.)* That but seeing, I should love her,
     And loving, woo, and wooing, she should grant?
COOKIE. *(To SCIENCE OFFICER.)* And will I persevere to en-
joy her?
TEMPEST. *(To BOSUN.)* And will I persevere to enjoy her?
TEMPEST/COOKIE. Ah me!!
SCIENCE OFFICER. *(To COOKIE.)* What passion hangs these
weights upon thy tongue?
TEMPEST & COOKIE. I cannot speak to her.
BOSUN. *(To TEMPEST.)* Yet she urged conference.
Oh Captain Tempest
SCIENCE OFFICER & BOSUN. Thou art all o'erthrown.
Miranda, or things weaker, master thee.

BOSUN. *(To TEMPEST.)* I know something about love.
SCIENCE OFFICER. *(To COOKIE.)* You've got to want it bad.
BOSUN. *(To TEMPEST.)* If that girl's into your blood,
SCIENCE OFFICER & BOSUN. Go out and get her.

(They sing "Tell Her".)

    SCIENCE OFFICER. *(Sings.)*
IF YOU WANT HER TO BE
THE VERY PART OF YOU
THAT MAKES YOU WANT TO BREATHE
HERE'S THE THING TO DO,
YOU'VE GOTTA
TELL HER THAT YOU'RE NEVER GONNA LEAVE HER
TELL HER THAT YOU'RE ALWAYS GONNA LOVE HER
TELL HER, TELL HER, TELL HER, TELL HER RIGHT NOW.

(Spoken—music vamps under.)

    TEMPEST. Damage report, damage report!
NAVIGATIONAL OFFICER. Klystron Generator malfunction!
BOSUN. Now hear this, now hear this! Damage control
Maintenance crew to level nineteen.
NAVIGATIONAL OFFICER. Condition Alpha!
BOSUN. Damage control
Damage control
To level nineteen
N, n, n, n, nineteen.
NAVIGATIONAL OFFICER. Condition Alpha. Condition Alpha!

(BOSUN blows whistle. The CREW take action stations.)

    SCIENCE OFFICER. *(Sings.)*
I KNOW SOMETHING ABOUT LOVE
YOU'VE GOT TO SHOW YOUR HAND
MAKE HER SEE THE MOON UP ABOVE
GO OUT AND GET IT.

IF YOU WANT HER SO
IT MAKES YOUR HEART SING OUT
IF YOU WANT HER TO
ONLY THINK OF YOU
THEN TELL HER THAT
YOU'RE NEVER GONNA LEAVE HER
    NAVIGATIONAL OFFICER. *(Spoken.)* Condition Alpha!
    SCIENCE OFFICER/COOKIE.
TELL HER THAT
    NAVIGATIONAL OFFICER. *(Spoken.)* Condition Alpha!
    SCIENCE OFFICER/COOKIE.
YOU'RE ALWAYS GONNA LOVE HER
    OMNES.
TELL HER, TELL HER, TELL HER
TELL HER RIGHT NOW
    TEMPEST. It's over to you Doc.
    Over to you Doc... What's up Doc!!!!
    SCIENCE OFFICER.
EVER SINCE THE WORLD BEGAN
IT'S BEEN THE SAME SINCE MAN
AND WOMAN WERE CREATED
THEY LOVE THEIR DESTINY
    COOKIE.
THEN WHY SHOULD TRUE LOVE BE SO
COMPLICATED?

(Spoken—in time to the music.)

    PROSPERO. I know... Reverse polarity!
    TEMPEST & BOSUN. Reverse polarity!!??
    SCIENCE OFFICER/COOKIE. Reverse polarity!
    BOSUN. The circuits'll never take it, Skip.
    TEMPEST. It's an old trick but it might just work.
    BOSUN. It's not logical.
    TEMPEST. Damn your logic, I've got lives to save.
    Reverse polarity!
    PROSPERO.
TELL HER...

TEMPEST.
TELL HER...
    PROSPERO.
TELL HER...
    BOSUN.
TELL HER...
    TEMPEST.
TELL HER...

(Spoken—music vamps under.)

    OMNES. Tell her right now!
    BOSUN. Reverse polarity!
    NAVIGATIONAL OFFICER. All passengers and crew adopt Polarity
Reversal Procedure. Reversing Polarity...

(The CAST and AUDIENCE perform the "Polarity Reversal Drill".)

    TEMPEST. Come on old girl... we know you can do it...
Don't let us down now.
    NAVIGATIONAL OFFICER. Overload! Overload! Press harder,
press harder!!

(The Klystron Generator explodes.)

    NAVIGATIONAL OFFICER. Polarity reversed!
    OMNES. Phew!
    TEMPEST. And the Klystron Generator?
    NAVIGATIONAL OFFICER. The Klystron Generator has fully
operational status.

(OMNES cheer.)

    SCIENCE OFFICER. *(Sings.)*
I KNOW SOMETHING ABOUT LOVE
YOU'VE GOT TO TAKE HER HAND
SHOW HER WHAT THE WORLD'S MADE OF.

SCIENCE OFFICER/COOKIE.
ONE KISS WILL PROVE IT.
IF YOU WANT HER TO BE
ALWAYS BY YOUR SIDE
TAKE HER HAND TONIGHT
SWALLOW YOUR FOOLISH PRIDE
TELL HER TELL HER
THAT YOU'RE NEVER GONNA LEAVE HER
TELL HER
THAT YOU'RE ALWAYS GONNA LOVE HER
TELL HER, TELL HER, TELL HER
TELL HER RIGHT NOW
   SCIENCE OFFICER.
OH YEAH
TELL HER THAT YOU'RE NEVER GONNA LEAVE HER
TELL HER THAT YOU'RE ALWAYS GONNA LOVE HER
TELL HER, TELL HER, TELL HER
TELL HER RIGHT NOW
TELL HER RIGHT NOW
TELL HER RIGHT NOW
TELL HER RIGHT
   COOKIE. Now!
   SCIENCE OFFICER. Now!
   TEMPEST. Now!

("She's Not There" underscores the following.)

   COOKIE. I am settled and bend up
Each corporal agent to this terrible feat.
Away and mock the time with fairest show.
False face must hide what the false heart doth know.

(COOKIE exits to steal the formula.)

   SCIENCE OFFICER. Prospero, Prospero, wherefore art thou Prospero?
("It's a Man's World" underscores the following.)

It must be by his death, and for my part
I know no personal cause to spurn him
But for the general. He has the drug:
How that might change his nature,
There's the question.
It is the bright day brings forth the adder
And therefore think him as a serpent's egg
Which hatched, would as his kind grow mischievous,
And kill him in his shell.
(Sings.)
THIS IS A MAN'S WORLD, BUT IT WOULDN'T BE NOTHING
WITHOUT A WOMAN ON THIS EARTH.

(SCIENCE OFFICER exits, ARIEL enters.)

ARIEL. Captain! Captain!
Well, that is that. I have repaired the crack
Upon the hull of this embattled craft
It seems the captain does know what he's at.
Although I sometimes wonder.

(To the opening bars of "Oh Pretty Woman" MIRANDA enters, wearing a very sexy dress and heavy makeup.)

TEMPEST.   What is that?
MIRANDA. Good morrow big boy!
ARIEL.   Mistress, is that you
Beneath that makeup and that strange attire?
TEMPEST. *(Aside.)* So fair and foul a wench I have not seen.
MIRANDA. It is, my Ariel, since I can't attract
The Captain with my youthful girlish charms
I thought a touch of slap might do the trick;
And a frock in Cosmopolitan,
An ancient tome that I have read of late
That shows you how to be sophisticate.
ARIEL. Oh madam, that will never work
For in that dress you'll miss. He'll not be
Swayed by haute couture.

MIRANDA. Honestly?

ARIEL. No shit!

And in strong proof of chastity he's armed
From such a silly ploy, he lives unharmed.

TEMPEST. What the Betelgeuse do you look like?

("This Is a Man's, Man's, Man's World" underscores the following.)

I never saw that painting you did need
And therefore to your face no painting set.
I found, or thought I found, she did excel
The barren tender of a poet's debt.
But now I find your charms are covered up.
Shall I compare thee to a Barbie Doll?
Is this a vision or a waking dream?
Go buy yourself a pot of cleansing cream.

ARIEL. *(Sings.)*

THIS IS A MAN'S WORLD.

MIRANDA. *(Sings.)*

BUT IT WOULDN'T BE NOTHING
WITHOUT A WOMAN ON THIS EARTH.

ARIEL. Young budding virgin, fair and fresh and sweet,
You have no use for such unsubtle traps.
I tell you miss and tell you truly too
I never saw a fresher gentlewoman.
Such war of white and red in your own cheeks.
What stars do spangle heaven with such beauty
As those two eyes become that heavenly face?

MIRANDA. Oh Ariel you are a constant friend
And for this sound advice I do thank you.
I wish the captain would make up his mind.
Oh spite, oh hell, I can't win either way.
So here I do abjure the love of men
That only brings us most uncalled for pain.
I want a robot man to hold me tight,
One that I can count on every single night.
He wouldn't run around like other guys.
I wouldn't have to listen to his alibis.

(MIRANDA sings "Robot Man". As she dances with ARIEL she taunts CAPTAIN TEMPEST.)

MIRANDA. *(Sings.)*
I WANT A ROBOT MAN TO CALL MY OWN
I'D NEVER HAVE TO WORRY THAT HE WOULDN'T PHONE
HE'D NEVER DANCE WITH ANYONE BUT ME
I'D JUST HAVE TO WIND HIM WITH MY ROBOT KEY.
I'D HAVE A STEADY DATE
SEVEN NIGHTS A WEEK.
 TEMPEST. Seven nights a week?
 MIRANDA.
AND WE WOULD NEVER FIGHT
'COS IT WOULD BE IMPOSSIBLE FOR HIM TO SPEAK.
DON'T WANT A REAL LIVE BOY TO GIVE ME GRIEF
ALWAYS MAKE ME CRY INTO MY HANKERCHIEF
SO IT'S A ROBOT MAN I'M DREAMING OF
BECAUSE I CAN DEPEND UPON A ROBOT LOVE
 ARIEL.
I'D HAVE A STEADY DATE
SEVEN NIGHTS A WEEK
 MIRANDA.
AND WE WOULD NEVER FIGHT
'COS IT WOULD BE IMPOSSIBLE FOR HIM TO SPEAK.
DON'T WANT A REAL LIVE BOY TO GIVE ME GRIEF
ALWAYS MAKE ME CRY INTO MY HANDKERCHIEF
SO IT'S A ROBOT MAN I'M DREAMING OF
BECAUSE I CAN DEPEND UPON A ROBOT LOVE
 ARIEL.
BECAUSE SHE CAN DEPEND UPON A ROBOT LOVE

*(At the end of the routine MIRANDA kisses ARIEL. COOKIE enters
with the stolen formula for the "X Factor".)*

COOKIE. I have done the deed and got the plans.
The "X-Factor" wanted by Gloria.
When she distills this mind expanding drug
My IQ will be right up there in lights
And then Miranda's bound to fancy me.
I should'na done it, but the die is cast
And to return were tedious as go o'er.

(COOKIE sees MIRANDA kissing ARIEL.)

O holy cow this is a sorry sight.

ARIEL. Sorry. Meaning, adjective, apologetic, full of grief or sorrow, compunctious, smitten... A foolish thought to say a sorry sight.

COOKIE. What vile perversions do you now perform
Against the laws of nature and of man?

ARIEL. Methinks thou hast the wrong end of the stick.
But may I ask what you have in your hand?
I think that it does not belong to you.

COOKIE. Mind your own business outsize cooking pot.
Just keep your distance Robot, watch your step.
Or I'll be forced to pull the plug on you.

ARIEL. Return the formula and I'll say naught
Or else a lesson you'll be swiftly taught.

Well get into that kitchen and rattle
Those pots and pans
Well get into that kitchen and rattle
Those pots and pans

(ARIEL sings "Shake, Rattle and Roll".)

WELL MAKE MY BREAKFAST, 'COS I FEEL HUNGRY MAN.
    COOKIE. *(To ARIEL.)*
YOU'RE GONNA SHAKE, RATTLE AND ROLL
SHAKE, RATTLE AND ROLL
SHAKE, RATTLE AND ROLL
SHAKE, RATTLE AND ROLL
WELL YOU'VE NEVER DONE NOTHING
TO SAVE YOUR TIN CAN SOUL.
(To MIRANDA.)
WEARING THAT DRESS WITH YOUR HAIR DONE UP SO NICE
WEARING THAT DRESS WITH YOUR HAIR DONE UP SO NICE
WELL YOUR LIPS ARE WARM, BUT YOUR HEART'S AS
COLD AS ICE

YOU'RE GONNA SHAKE, RATTLE AND ROLL

SHAKE, RATTLE AND ROLL
SHAKE, RATTLE AND ROLL
SHAKE, RATTLE AND ROLL
WELL YOU NEVER DO NOTHING
TO SAVE YOUR TIN CAN SOUL.
    CREW.
SHAKE, RATTLE AND ROLL
SHAKE, RATTLE AND ROLL
SHAKE, RATTLE AND ROLL
SHAKE, RATTLE AND ROLL

(Instrumental. COOKIE and ARIEL fight. This fight is choreographed as a jive routine. At the end of the fight ARIEL retrieves the formula and eats it. COOKIE draws his ray gun.)

    COOKIE. Hold it trash can, I beat you to the draw.
    ARIEL. I'm sorry, sir, the formula's no more.
    COOKIE. You stupid scrapheap, now look what you've done:
Swallowed the secret of the Doctor's drug.
(ARIEL starts to malfunction.)
Hey, what will we do now, metallic pest?
    ARIEL. I read, I mark, and inwardly digest.
    MIRANDA. Help, Father, my derang—ed drone has flipped.
    COOKIE. Oh grow up girl! The goddamn thing is ripped.
    PROSPERO. You blocks, he's stoned, a worse than senseless thing!
My whole life's work has just gone down his throat.
I will have revenge on you both
That all the world shall... I will do such things,
What they are yet, I know not, but they shall be
The terrors of the earth.
("Gloria" underscores the following.)
Oh horror, horror, horror. Tongue nor heart
Cannot conceive nor name thee.
    BOSUN. What's the matter?
    NAVIGATIONAL OFFICER. Oh Captain, Captain, there's another beep
Upon my radar screen, the very shape

That signified th' approach of that space gorgon.
BOSUN. Quick Doctor, pull yourself together please.
Your robot's phasers are our one defense.
COOKIE. It's no good Bosun, the damn thing's OD'd.

(The underscore stopes. Four huge drum beats are heard, as if giant footsteps are approaching. On each drum beat everything in the spaceship rattles. The underscore builds again.)

NAVIGATIONAL OFFICER. *(Sings.)*
HERE IT COMES
HERE IT COMES
    TEMPEST. Put up the force field.
    OMNES.
COMING UP THE STAIRS.
    BOSUN. Force field engaged.
    NAVIGATIONAL OFFICER.
HERE IT COMES.
    TEMPEST. Activate the photon shields.
(Synthesizer effect.)
    OMNES.
COMING THROUGH THE DOOR.
    NAVIGATIONAL OFFICER.
HERE IT COMES.

(The SCIENCE OFFICER enters, overpowers COOKIE and takes his ray gun. The underscore stops.)

PROSPERO. Gloria!
SCIENCE OFFICER. And so, dear Prospero, we meet again.
BOSUN. Put down that ray gun madam, if you please.
COOKIE. You mustn't do it.
SCIENCE OFFICER.   Shut up Cookie. Freeze!
PROSPERO. Gloria, no more, begone I say.

(Underscore starts.)

SCIENCE OFFICER. You are a man of sin, whom destiny
That hath to instrument this other world
And what is on it, which never surfeited space,
Hath caused to belch upon this planet.
He's told you all, no doubt, how I did act
Those many years ago back on our Earth,
Of how I did set him adrift in space
And put him in an orbit of no hope.
The fool, the fool, as if his ape brain could
Contain the wonders of that marv'lous drug,
His true creation, "Telegenesis",
His new found science, with no instrument.
I loved him, and I warned him what would be.
PROSPERO. Enough! Oh Gloria, please say no more.
SCIENCE OFFICER. Now you must face the truth my Prospero.
You have created monsters from the Id.

(Underscore stops.)

TEMPEST. What is this Id? Can someone tell me, please?

(Underscore starts.)

SCIENCE OFFICER. Of course. It's what was once used to de-
scribe
The basis of man's own subconscious mind.
TEMPEST. Monsters from the Id? I still don't see.
SCIENCE OFFICER. The "X Factor" released his genius brain
To transmit matter where he wanted it.
But he forgot one deadly danger, sir:
Subconscious hate and lust for destruction.

(Underscore stops.)

TEMPEST. A monster from your subconscious? My God!

(Underscore starts.)

SCIENCE OFFICER. He knew the dangers. He created it
And though he hoped that it would help mankind
He did forget the brute subconscious mind.
PROSPERO. The mind, the mind. It is so primitive.
I have unlocked the devil in my soul.
And set it free to do as it would wish.
To take revenge, to plunder and to kill.
SCIENCE OFFICER. There will be blood I said, there will be
blood.
Stones have been known to move and trees to speak.
PROSPERO. Kill the physicist
And the fee bestow upon the foul disease.
SCIENCE OFFICER. I did what we both knew I had to do
So long ago in our laboratory.
But what I did, I did for love of you,
Our daughter and for children yet unborn.
PROSPERO. It is myself that lurks outside the door.
(The underscore stops. PROSPERO collapses. Suddenly he is very
calm.)
Now my charms are all o'erthrown
And what strength I have's'mine own.
Prospero now ends his tale
To ensure his project fails
(The introduction to "Go Now" begins.)
Which was to please. Now I want
Science to enforce, art to enchant;
And my ending is despair,
Unless I be relieved by prayer.
And as you from crimes would pardoned be
Let your indulgence set me free.

(The SCIENCE OFFICER sings "Go Now".)

SCIENCE OFFICER.
WE'VE ALREADY SAID GOODBYE
SINCE YOU GOT TO GO
OH YOU BETTER GO NOW
GO NOW, GO NOW, GO NOW

BEFORE YOU SEE ME CRY
I DON'T WANT YOU TO TELL ME
JUST WHAT YOU INTEND TO DO NOW
AND HOW MANY TIMES DO I HAVE TO TELL YOU
DARLING, DARLING
I'M STILL IN LOVE WITH YOU NOW, OH
WE'VE ALREADY SAID SO LONG
I DON'T WANT TO SEE YOU GO
OH YOU BETTER GO NOW
GO NOW, GO NOW, GO NOW
DON'T YOU EVEN TRY
TELLING ME YOU DIDN'T REALY WANT IT
TO END THIS WAY
'COS DARLING, DARLING, CAN'T YOU SEE
I WANT YOU TO STAY. OH OH, OH, OH
*(Instrumental. PROSPERO bids a tender farewell to MIRANDA and
     GLORIA.)*
SINCE YOU GOT TO GO
OH YOU BETTER GO NOW
GO NOW, GO NOW, GO NOW
BEFORE YOU SEE ME CRY
I DON'T WANT YOU TO TELL ME
 JUST WHAT YOU INTEND TO DO NOW
AND HOW MANY TIMES DO I HAVE TO TELL YOU
I'M STILL IN LOVE WITH YOU NOW. OH
(PROSPERO exits.)
OH I DON'T WANT TO SEE YOU GO
BUT DARLING, YOU'D BETTER GO NOW

    SCIENCE OFFICER. What say'st you of him now? Come Captain, speak.

("Don't Let Me Be Misunderstood" underscores the following.)

    TEMPEST. Why ma'am, he did bestride this narrow world
Like a colossus, and we petty men
Walked under his huge legs and peeped about
To find ourselves dishonorable graves.

Men sometimes can be masters of their fates:
The fault, dear Gloria lies not in the stars
But in ourselves that we are underlings.

(From outside the space ship we hear the ghostly voice of DOCTOR PROSPERO.)

PROSPERO. *(Sings off.)*
WELL I'M JUST A SOUL WHOSE INTENTIONS WERE GOOD
OH LORD, PLEASE DON'T LET ME BE MISUNDERSTOOD.
    SCIENCE OFFICER. Beware the Ids that March!
    MIRANDA. Break heart, I prithee break.
    SCIENCE OFFICER. Look up my love. Vex not his ghost, oh let him pass.
    TEMPEST. He hates him that would upon the rack of this
Tough world stretch him out longer.
    SCIENCE OFFICER. He is gone indeed.
    TEMPEST. The wonder is he hath endured so long
He but usurped his life. Come let's depart.
    SCIENCE OFFICER. The weight of this sad hour we must obey
Speak what we feel, not what we ought to say.
    TEMPEST. Yes all the faith, the virtue of my heart,
The object and the pleasure of mine eye
Are only yours.
    MIRANDA.   Oh Captain of my dreams.

(TEMPEST and MIRANDA embrace.)

    SCIENCE OFFICER. Fair lovers you are fortunately met.
Of this discourse we will hear more on Earth.
My lost one now is found. Ye gods look down
And from your sacred vials pour your graces
Upon these lover's heads.
    TEMPEST.   Why thank you Ma'am.

(MIRANDA and TEMPEST kiss. The intro to "Only the Lonely" underscores the following.)

COOKIE. See how vilely they do kiss and court
Here is my hand and here I firmly vow
Never to woo her more
But do forswear her as one unworthy
Of all the former favors
That I have fondly flattered her withal
BOSUN. You must be wise hereafter and seek for grace.
COOKIE. *(Sings.)*
ONLY THE LONELY
THERE GOES MY BABY
THERE GOES MY HEART
  BOSUN.
SHE'S GONE FOREVER
  COOKIE.
SO FAR APART
BUT ONLY THE LONELY KNOW WHY
I CRY.
  CREW.
ONLY THE LONELY
  TEMPEST. A glooming peace this morning with it brings
This lowly cook for sorrow hangs his head
His theft was at the cause of these sad things
Should he be pardoned or be punish—ed?

(The AUDIENCE pass sentence.)

  TEMPEST. The quality of your mercy is not strain'd
It droppeth as the gentle rain from Heaven
Upon the place beneath.
  COOKIE. 'Tis very true O wise and upright judge!
How much more elder art thou than thy looks!
  TEMPEST. The oldest have borne most . We that are young
Shall never see so much or live so long.

(Panic breaks out on the flight deck. On the video screen we see the surface of the planet breaking up.)

  NAVIGATIONAL OFFICER. Quick! Help! Our sensors must

be on the blink.

    I have seen tempests when the scalding winds
    Have rev'd the knotty oaks; and I have seen
    The ambitious ocean rage and swell and foam
    To be exalted with the threatening clouds;
    But never till today, never till now.
    Did I go through a tempest dropping fire.
    Either there is civil strife in heaven
    Or else this world too saucy with the gods
    Incenses them to send destruction.
    ARIEL. If you'll permit. This all seems logical.
    If Prospero's Id created that monster
    Then this most beauteous planet surely is
    His Super-Ego.
    TEMPEST.   I don't understand!
    ARIEL. Well just as Prospero destroyed himself
    By committing galactic suicide,
    Then this same planet, created as 'twas
    By his own Super-Ego, does the same.

(The intro to "Born to be Wild" begins.)

    TEMPEST. Prepare for take-off; quickly we must go
    And put as many light years as we can
    Between us and this self-destructive star.
    TEMPEST. *(Sings.)*
GET THE MOTORS RUNNING
    BOSUN.
HEAD OUT ON THE SKYWAY
    COOKIE.
LOOKING FOR ADVENTURE
AND WHATEVER COMES OUR WAY
    TEMPEST.
YOU KNOW WE'RE GONNA MAKE IT HAPPEN
TAKE YOUR GIRL IN A LOVE EMBRACE
(TEMPEST embraces MIRANDA.)
FIRE ALL OF THOSE GUNS AT ONCE
AND EXPLODE INTO SPACE.

(Spoken—music vamps under.)

    SCIENCE OFFICER. Iambics functioning.
    BOSUN. Pentameters locked in.
    SCIENCE OFFICER. Hyperboles all off the scale.
    BOSUN. R.S.C. jettisoned.
    TEMPEST. Red alert, red alert! All crew to action stations!
    NAVIGATIONAL OFFICER. 10, 9, 8, 7, 6, 5, 4, 3, 2, 1

(The CREW segue into "Wipe Out". On the video we see the space-ship taking off and flying through space.)

    NAVIGATIONAL OFFICER. We are now cruising in hyperdrive and have
    Achieved a no-emergency scenario.
    MIRANDA. Oh mighty father, dost thou lie so low?
    Are all they conquests, glories, triumphs spoils
    Shrunk to this little measure? Fare thee well.
    TEMPEST. All that glitters is not gold;
    Often have you heard that told.
    (But now of his brave end the world will know.)
    SCIENCE OFFICER. Farewell my love, live long and Prospero!

(On the video we see the planet D'Ilyria explode.)

    MIRANDA. Sound drums and trumpets! Farewell sour annoy,
(The music stops.)
    For here I hope, begins our lasting joy.

(MIRANDA sings "Mr. Spaceman".)

    MIRANDA.
WOKE UP THIS MORNING WITH LIGHT IN MY EYES
AND THEN REALIZED IT WAS STILL DARK OUTSIDE
IT WAS A LIGHT COMING DOWN FROM THE SKY
I DON'T KNOW WHO OR WHY
MUST BE THOSE STRANGERS THAT COME EVERY NIGHT

THOSE SAUCER-SHAPED LIGHTS GET PEOPLE UPTIGHT
LEAVE BLUE-GREEN FOOTPRINTS THAT GLOW IN THE
    DARK
I HOPE THEY GET HOME ALL RIGHT.
    OMNES.
HEY MR. SPACEMAN
WON'T YOU PLEASE TAKE ME ALONG
I WON'T DO ANYTHING WRONG
HEY MR.. SPACEMAN
WON'T YOU PLEASE TAKE ME ALONG
FOR A RIDE
    MIRANDA.
WOKE UP THIS MORNING
I WAS FEELING QUITE WEIRD
HAD FLIES IN MY BEER
AND MY TOOTHPASTE WAS SMEARED.
OVER MY WINDOW THEY'D WRITTEN MY NAME
SAID SO LONG WE'LL SEE YOU AGAIN
    OMNES.
HEY MR. SPACEMAN
WON'T YOU PLEASE TAKE ME ALONG
I WON'T DO ANYTHING WRONG
    MIRANDA.
I'M IN LOVE WITH YOU MR. SPACEMAN
TAKE A LOOK AT HIM HE'S MY SPACEMAN
WON'T YOU TAKE ME NOW
    OMNES.
HEY MR. SPACEMAN
WON'T YOU PLEASE TAKE ME ALONG
FOR A RIDE
HEY MR. SPACEMAN
WON'T YOU PLEASE TAKE ME ALONG
FOR A RIDE.

(BLACKOUT. The Video comes on.)

NEWSCASTER. *(On video.)* If we shadows have offended,
Think but this, and all is mended:
That you have but slumbered here
While these visions did appear
And this weak and idle theme
No more yielding but a dream.
Gentles do not reprehend:
If you pardon we will mend.
And, as I am an honest Scot,
If we have unearned luck
Now to 'scape the critic's tongue
We will make amends ere long;
else this man a liar call.
So goodnight unto you all.
Give us your hands, please do feel free,
Take it away!
NAVIGATIONAL OFFICER. One, two, three.

(PROSPERO enters. He sings "The Monster Mash")

PROSPERO. *(Sings.)*
I WAS WORKING IN MY LAB, LATE LAST NIGHT,
WHEN MY EYES BEHELD AN EVIL SIGHT.
FOR MY MONSTER FROM THE ID BEGAN TO RISE
AND SUDDENLY, TO MY SURPRISE
   OMNES.
HE DID THE MASH
   PROSPERO.
HE DID THE MONSTER MASH
   OMNES.
THE MONSTER MASH
   PROSPERO.
IT WAS A GRAVEYARD SMASH
   OMNES.
HE DID THE MASH
   PROSPERO.
IT CAUGHT ON IN A FLASH

OMNES.
THE MONSTER MASH
   PROSPERO.
THEY DID THE MONSTER MASH
   PROSPERO.
THE SCENE WAS ROCKING AND ROLLING TO THE SOUND
IGOR ON CHAINS BACKED BY HIS BAYING HOUNDS
THE COFFIN MAKERS WERE ABOUT TO ARRIVE
WITH THEIR VOCAL GROUP THE CRYPT KICKER FIVE

(The monster tentacles fly in. PROSPERO dances with them.)

   OMNES.
HE DID THE MASH
   PROSPERO.
HE DID THE MONSTER MASH
   OMNES.
THE MONSTER MASH
   PROSPERO
IT WAS A GRAVEYARD SMASH
   OMNES.
HE DID THE MASH
   PROSPERO.
IT CAUGHT ON IN A FLASH
   OMNES.
THEY DID THE MASH
   PROSPERO.
THEY DID THE MONSTER MASH.

(The tentacles fly out. "The Monster Mash" segues into "Great Balls of Fire".)

   COOKIE.
YOU SHAKE MY NERVES AND YOU RATTLE MY BRAIN.
YOUR KIND OF LOVE COULD DRIVE A MAN INSANE.
YOU BROKE MY WILL, OH WHAT A THRILL
GOODNESS GRACIOUS, GREAT BALLS OF FIRE.

I HAD A LOVE AND I THOUGHT IT WAS FUNNY.
YOU CAME ALONG AND MOVED ME HONEY.
YOU CHANGED MY MIND, LOVE'S FINE
GOODNESS GRACIOUS, GREAT BALLS OF FIRE.

KISS ME BABY
OOH, THAT FEELS GOOD
HUG ME BABY
I WANNA LOVE YOU LIKE A LOVER SHOULD
YOU'RE FINE, SO KIND
WANNA TELL THE WORLD THAT YOU'RE MINE, MINE, MINE.

I CHEW MY NAILS AND I TWIDDLE MY THUMBS
I'M REALLY NERVOUS, BUT THIS SURE IS FUN.
YOU BROKE MY WILL, OH WHAT A THRILL
GOODNESS GRACIOUS, GREAT BALLS OF FIRE.

(Guitar solo.)

KISS ME BABY
OOH, THAT FEELS GOOD
HUG ME BABY
I WANNA LOVE YOU LIKE A LOVER SHOULD
YOU'RE FINE, SO KIND
WANNA TELL THE WORLD THAT YOU'RE MINE, MINE,MINE.

I CHEW MY NAILS AND I TWIDDLE MY THUMBS.
I'M REALLY NERVOUS, BUT THIS SURE IS FUN.
YOU BROKE MY WILL, OH WHAT A THRILL
GOODNESS GRACIOUS, GREAT BALLS OF FIRE.
GOODNESS GRACIOUS, GREAT BALLS OF FIRE.

Big rock and roll finish. Blackout followed by curtain calls.)

END OF PLAY

OTHER TITLES AVAILABLE FROM SAMUEL FRENCH

THE AWESOME 80s PROM
Ken Davenport and The Class of '89

Interactive Comedy / 11m, 8f / Unit Set
The Awesome 80s Prom is a brand new blast-from-the-past party in the style of *Tony 'n Tina's Wedding* and *The Donkey Show,* set at Wanaget High's Senior Prom...in 1989! All your favorite characters from your favorite '80s movies are at the Prom, from the Captain of the Football Team to the Asian Exchange Student, from the Geek to the hottie Head Cheerleader, and they're all competing for Prom King and Queen. And just like on "American Idol", the audience decides who wins! Come back in time and join the breakdance circle or just sit back and watch the '80s drama unfold.

WINNER! 2006 IMPROV THEATER AWARD
"BEST INTERACTIVE SHOW"

OTHER TITLES AVAILABLE FROM SAMUEL FRENCH

RUTHLESS! THE MUSICAL
Book and Lyrics by Joal Paley
Music by Marvin Laird

Musical spoof / 1m, 5f or 6f / Unit set
Eight year old Tina Denmark knows she was born to play Pippi
Longstocking, and she will do anything to win the part in her
school musical. Anything includes murdering the leading lady!
This aggressively outrageous musical hit garnered rave reviews
during its long Off Broadway run.

"A spoof that has enough absurd plot twists and multiple
identities to fill several old movies.... The fun comes from the
sheer brazenness."
— *New York Times*

"Wild amusement."
— *New York Post*

"A wonderfully smart and funny send up of every Broadway
brat from *Gypsy* to *The Bad Seed*... loaded with campy wit and
charm."
— *Variety*

OTHER TITLES AVAILABLE FROM SAMUEL FRENCH

GUTENBERG! THE MUSICAL!
Scott Brown and Anthony King

2m / Musical Comedy

In this two-man musical spoof, a pair of aspiring playwrights perform a backers' audition for their new project - a big, splashy musical about printing press inventor Johann Gutenberg. With an unending supply of enthusiasm, Bud and Doug sing all the songs and play all the parts in their crass historical epic, with the hope that one of the producers in attendance will give them a Broadway contract - fulfilling their ill-advised dreams.

"A smashing success!"
— *New York Times*

"Brilliantly realized and side-splitting!
— *New York Magazine*

"There are lots of genuine laughs in Gutenberg!"
— *New York Post*

OTHER TITLES AVAILABLE FROM SAMUEL FRENCH

THE SPITFIRE GRILL
Music and Book by James Valcq
Lyrics and Book by Fred Alley
Based on the film by Lee David Zlotoff

Musical Drama / 3m, 4f / Unit Set

A feisty parolee follows her dreams, based on a page from an old travel book, to a small town in Wisconsin and finds a place for herself working at Hannah's Spitfire Grill. It is for sale but there are no takers for the only eatery in the depressed town, so newcomer Percy suggests to Hannah that she raffle it off. Entry fees are one hundred dollars and the best essay on why you want the grill wins. Soon, mail is arriving by the wheelbarrow full and things are definitely cookin' at the Spitfire Grill.

"An abundance of warmth, spirit and goodwill!...Some of the most engaging and instantly infectious melodies I've heard in an original musical in some time."
USA Today

"A soul satisfying...work of theatrical resourcefulness. A compelling story that flows with grace and carries the rush of anticipation. The story moves, the characters have many dimensions and their transformations are plausible and moving. The musical is freeing. It is penetrated by honesty and it glows."
– *The New York Times*